MEMORY FIELD

Memory Field

A Travelogue of Forgetting

Eric Tyler Benick

Long Day Press
Chicago

Copyright © 2024 Eric Tyler Benick
Published by Long Day Press
Chicago, Il 60647
LongDayPress.com
@LongDayPress

All rights reserved. Parts of this book may be reproduced in brief passages for reviewing or educational purposes, provided the Author and Publisher are acknowledged in the reproduction. Why would you steal from us?

ISBN 978-1-950987-44-3 (Paperback Edition)
ISBN 979-8-330359-62-2 (eBook Edition)
Library of Congress Control Number: 2024937946

Cover and Layout Design by Joshua Bohnsack
Photos by Eric Tyler Benick
Proofreading by Zoe Seipp

First Edition
LDP 31

For Tawni.

*I deepened myself but I don't believe in myself
because thought is invented.*
—*Clarice Lispector*

My illness don't come with no remedy.
—*Doja Cat*

We visit Modigliani in Père-Lachaise.
Proust, Piaf, Delacroix, Apollinaire.
You can see my leaves splayed across
them — my artichoke gratitude.

In Mondello, we try to find my mother's home but find the beach instead. We caper in the Italian sand — our briny buds unbloomed. A man with no teeth selling coconuts. The taxi back to Palermo nearly hits a couple on their Vespa. In the center of the city, I feel like Florida.

The farmer, Mauro, who is not a farmer but a cellist, hands me an axe. I break wood while Tawni irrigates the vines. It's delicious, right? All this dry sun? How bad it feels?

At six a.m. no one is awake in Bologna.
I run the long portico to San Luca,
past the six hundred and sixty-six
arches. At the top, I am a weak carrot
in the face of something ineffable.
Not God because God isn't a real
word. But the dawn light over the
orange tile and my heart like a potato
battery and trees like trees aren't trees
but swaths of greenbrown paint.

We stay with an old friend in Lugano where there isn't much to do but stand around and say, *Oh fuck* at how pretty everything is. I finally get to use the word *fjord* in direct relation to my surroundings, even though I am nowhere near Scandinavia.

Even when I try to be candid I make
up the small details.

Every pizzeria owner in Naples resembles my father. The cobblestones are alive with glass. Garages filled with garbage. Somehow the metro is spotless. A fresh pigeon splatters before our feet. We buy a bottle of wine for a euro and expect to go blind. The ferry arrives late. It takes an hour for them to unload the contraband.

I see my first white widow while digging up the rotten wood of a pigpen. Covered in shit and rust, I am passed a carafe of orange wine. I learn about fermentation and can't help but empathize.

I read Reverdy from a small window in Ménilmontant. I watch a man in jelly sandals unload cantaloupe into a market. We listen to Archie Shepp through laptop speakers. Tawni asks me how I feel about onions. I say *yes, please*.

Mauro keeps his cello in the same room as his wine and prosciutto — the only room on the farm with temperature control. I look at the golden legs of meat hanging on the wall. I ask him what will become of the pig. *She will live*, he tells me, *but I will eat her children.*

We make enough risotto in Palermo to last a week. We watch Pasolini's *Salò* without subtitles. We also watch Sandler's *The Waterboy* without subtitles. Both are indiscernible, but move me.

No one can deny the beauty of Notre-Dame. No one can also deny the ugliness that built it.

I am obstreperous in the morning heat. Just look at me putting on my pants, my bat wings fluttering, my eyes full of mucus.

Tense does not create time. It is only the reality of its utterance.

In Brooklyn, I dream of Clarice Lispector — all of her, a topaz bird. I touch the painted window of a church and hum. I am filled with so much love I am certain it is death.

Every mirror in the world has forsaken me. My likeness is stolen and distorted. I've never trusted glass, what it milks of us, always severe and quicksilver.

Fuck you, Nashville. Your perverted infrastructure. Your gonads of lower Broadway. Your fake accents as bad as your fake Athena. I denounce you as you denounced me. I consort now with the apparitions of Elliston Place. I sleep in their memories where we bask in the amber resin of your angels.

Fuck you, Portland. Your flaccid enterprise. The unhoused you could have covered. The debts you've made in the manufacture of your own image. Whenever I return, everyone is hurting even more than before. Some Lacanian cryptobro mansplains sex work to a dancer at Sassy's. Some trustfund Marxist tries to disarm everyone with rhetoric only to displace another family. Some manbun personality pisses in my cup again and calls it beer.

If I tell the truth it is because I am lacking.

I read books while crossing busy intersections. Bowery and Houston. 14th and 4th. Jaywalking Atlantic Ave. The day I get hit I'll become a New Yorker.

The hunks of Barceloneta do pull-ups in their Speedos. I know I am a stranger because I'm the only one watching. I buy two beers for a euro and drink them like water.

I'm not convinced of much more than *thing* and *place*. The rest, I think, is circumstance, which is still the solution of the two. You can algorithm *thing/place* infinitely. Place is not special. Neither is thing. They are both conditions. *What* we are is as much our condition as *where* we are. I've *thing/placed* my entire way here and look at me, I turned out fine.

Cagliari stacks upon itself. Each direction an eventual misdirection. Sometimes the way to go down is up. The inverse is also true, as is the opposite. A still-crusaded place, domes of old mosques rising over Spanish tile. Piazzas that still smell of blood. Street after street of erasure. You can try to conquer an architecture, but the past has a clever way of recurrence.

If I (*thing*) sit on the terrace (*place/thing*) in my underwear (*thing*) and enjoy the air (*thing/place*) and an espresso (*thing*), how much blood (*thing*) is now on my hands (*things/place*)? My lips? Indwelling? Digested?

And yet, out of the stone, oranges.

Standing in the Prado, crowded around Bosch's *Garden of Earthly Delights*, I am the entity with flowers from its anus.

Cypress and I get drunk in the West Village, first at Julius', then at Zinc, then at Formerly Crows where we shouldn't drink anymore, but we do, plus there are billiards and more friends. The walk to W 4th is brilliant and messy, stepping over the putrid gutters aglitter with Manhattan. I pass out on the D train and wake up at 205th thinking, reverently, about Slick Rick.

YOUNG ENGLISH POET

Low in the empty Roman cistern, I sing the famous refrain of *baby back ribs*. It plumes up the walls in Gregorian echo. What sounds of *barbecue sauce* could as easily be the belly of God. Their edifying answer.

This Grave
contains all that was Mortal
of a
YOUNG ENGLISH POET
who
on his Death Bed
in the Bitterness of his Heart
at the Malicious Power of his Enemies
Desired
these Words to be engraven on his Tomb Stone

Here lies One
Whose Name was writ in Water
Feb 24ᵗʰ 1821

Sometimes I think of myself as stable, but can barely withstand the turbulence of passing through a soft cloud.

30,000 feet above the Iberian coast and I'm still below the cypress and stone pine eating the grass off the grave of John Keats.

YOUNG ENGLISH POET

Here lies One
Whose Name was writ in Water
Feb 24 1821

This world isn't nearly as strange as it is impossible. Watch your hand carefully and the digits double. Behold the space you occupy and notice it's likely somewhere your body isn't.

Every day I awaken I am certain is invented. My components all wrong. My every heart a wrench dropped from the water of my skull to the ceiling of my feet.

I turn thirty in Montreal with a broken ass. I hobble around on ice feeling paranoid as if on the verge of waking. In a bookstore by McGill I buy a copy of Marcuse's *Negations*, Oppen's *Meaning: A Life* and Duncan's *Bending the Bow*. Tawni and I find a dark pub and drink while the snow comes down. Across from us, a small pink house with its porchlight on.

I sense I have become entirely object.
My brickwork brutalist and elegant.
I tickle the sky and laugh at my ephemerae.

On Mount Royal I am onion-sweet.
Almost pure idiot. I macerate and age
instantly.

In Mile End, I consort with Lispector again. She is bear-heavy and full of rubies. I press her for clarity and she tongues my third eye like a cockroach. Twilight suddenly scrambles like internet.

Quietly, on the back deck, a raccoon unfolds his hand. I know he is mendacious, but I trust him completely.

In the gray Mazda passing through Carroll Gardens, I listen to Fred Moten correct Brian Lehrer's definition of improvisation. Improvisation, Moten says, is not an aesthetic inquiry into the unknown future but a spirited rumination of the past. The eminent memory excavates its mystery live and we shiver beneath what surfaces. When the segment ends I say something stupid to Tawni about money.

Caffeinated in Trastevere, I read Tawni my notes on an essay I've titled "Cataclysmic Pussy Ritual." I cannot contain my excitement when I articulate the evidence of cultural hegemony I've found convincing in the controversy of Cardi B and Megan Thee Stallion's sensational hit "WAP." Tawni tells me my concept is problematic. The percolator screams over us both like a petulant child.

I return to Gramsci in Il Cimitero Acattolico. The small tree out of his shoulder. Red flowers across his belly. A body no longer body but an interpellation of death. Fugues of wind across my scalp. To think *Here I am* is Abrahamic and trite, and yet, I am moved by its persistence. Evidence of my little life.

A wild mushroom emanates from the kitchen. Erik Satie threads the air sparsely. Our cat licks his ass under the Christmas tree. Outside, light rain, the sky a gray slipper. I type this up not to remember it, but to let go of it.

Somewhere between states of cognition, I could almost hear my old voice singing his opals of innocence.

Eric Tyler Benick is the author of the poetry collection *the fox hunts* (Beautiful Days, 2023) along with several chapbooks. With Nick Rossi, he runs Ursus Americanus Press, a publisher of smaller poetic works. His recent work has appeared or is forthcoming in *Bennington Review, Copper Nickle, The Harvard Advocate, Southeast Review,* and *Tagvverk*. He lives in Brooklyn.

Long Day Press

Recommended Titles

DESOLATION
frankie baby
Essay
ISBN: 9781950987450 • $14

In Between My Bodies
Emily Capers
Essays
ISBN: 9781950987467 • $14

In Memory of James Wright, Whose Poem I Ate
Tyler Cain Lacy
Novella
ISBN: 9781950987498 • $16

How to Adjust to the Dark
Rebecca Van Laer
Novella
ISBN: 9781950987207 • $16

LongDayPress.com @LongDayPress

www.ingramcontent.com/pod-product-compliance
Lightning Source LLC
Chambersburg PA
CBHW061811070526
44586CB00024B/2810